Workbook
for James Clear's
Atomic Habits

A Practical Exercises for Transformative Change

Copyright © 2022 by Reed's Publishers
All rights reserved. No part of this book may be used or reproduced in any form whatsoever without written permission except in the case of brief quotations in critical articles or reviews.

This workbook's objective is not to instantly alter all of your behaviors. The objective should be to develop one simple habit that will significantly improve your life. You may work on your next habit whenever your current habit starts to become established by printing a fresh copy of this workbook. Over time, these little adjustments will add up and completely change your life!

WORKBOOK

Introduction

- What are some of your biggest struggles with building good habits or breaking bad ones?

_____
_____
_____
_____
_____
_____
_____
_____
_____
_____
_____
_____
_____
_____
_____

- How do you think your life would improve if you were able to make small improvements every day?

_____
_____
_____
_____
_____

Chapter 1:
The Surprising Power of Atomic Habits

- Write down your definition of an "atomic habit."

_____
_____
_____
_____
_____
_____
_____
_____
_____
_____
_____
_____
_____
_____
_____
_____
_____

- What are some of the benefits of focusing on small habits rather than big, sweeping changes?

_____
_____
_____
_____
_____
_____
_____

- Think about a small habit you could start today that would move you closer to one of your goals. Write it down and commit to doing it for the next 30 days.

Chapter 2:
How Your Habits Shape Your Identity (and Vice Versa)

- Reflect on your current identity. How would you describe yourself?

_____
_____
_____
_____
_____
_____
_____
_____
_____
_____
_____
_____
_____
_____
_____
_____

- What are some habits that are in line with your desired identity? What are some that are not?

_____
_____
_____
_____
_____
_____
_____
_____
_____

- Identify one habit you could change that would help you better align with your desired identity. Write it down and make a plan for how you will start implementing it.

Chapter 3:
How to Build Better Habits in 4 Simple Steps

- Identify a habit you want to build using the 4-step process outlined in this chapter: Cue, Craving, Response, and Reward.

- Write down each step of the process as it relates to your habit.

- Think about potential roadblocks or challenges you might face when trying to build this habit. How will you overcome them?

Chapter 4:
The Secret to Better Habits? Make Them Easy

- What is the "2-minute rule," and how can it help you build new habits?

- Identify a habit you've been struggling to build and think about how you can make it easier using the 2-minute rule.

- Write down your plan for implementing this habit using the 2-minute rule.

Chapter 5:
The Role of Environment in Habit Formation

- Reflect on the environments you spend the most time in. How do they support or hinder your habits?

_____

- Think about one environment you could optimize to better support a habit you want to build.

_____

Write down your plan for optimizing this environment and making it more conducive to your habit-building goals.

Chapter 6:
How to Find and Fix the Causes of Your Bad Habits

- Identify one bad habit you want to break.

_____
_____
_____
_____
_____
_____
_____
_____
_____
_____
_____
_____
_____
_____
_____
_____
_____
_____

- Use the "5 Whys" technique to uncover the root cause of this habit.

_____
_____
_____
_____
_____
_____
_____
_____
_____
_____
_____
_____
_____

- Write down your plan for addressing this root cause and replacing the bad habit with a good one.

Chapter 7:
Designing Your Environment to Make Success Inevitable

- Identify one habit you want to build and one you want to break.

- Think about how you can design your environment to make success inevitable for each of these habits.

- Write down your plan for optimizing your environment to support these habits.

Chapter 8:
Making It Obvious

- Identify a habit you want to build and think about how you can make it more obvious.

_____
_____
_____
_____
_____
_____
_____
_____
_____
_____
_____
_____
_____
_____
_____
_____
_____

- Write down your plan for using cues to make this habit more visible and prominent in your daily life.

_____
_____
_____
_____
_____
_____
_____
_____

Chapter 9:
Making It Attractive

- Identify a habit you want to build and think about how you can make it more attractive.

_____
_____
_____
_____
_____
_____
_____
_____
_____
_____
_____
_____
_____
_____
_____
_____
_____

- Write down your plan for adding elements of pleasure or satisfaction to this habit to make it more appealing.

_____
_____
_____
_____
_____
_____
_____
_____

Chapter 10:
Making It Easy

- Identify a habit you want to build and think about how you can make it easier.

- Write down your plan for using the 2-minute rule or other techniques to reduce the friction associated with this habit.

Chapter 11:
Making It Satisfying

- Identify a habit you want to build and think about how you can make it more satisfying.

___

- Write down your plan for adding a sense of immediate gratification or reward to this habit to make it more enjoyable.

___

Chapter 12:
Advanced Tactics for Sticking to Your Habits

- Think about a habit you've tried to build in the past but struggled to stick with.

- Review the advanced tactics outlined in this chapter and identify one or two that you think could help you stick to this habit in the future.

- Write down your plan for using these tactics to overcome any obstacles and stay committed to your habit.

Chapter 13:
How to Make Habits a Core Part of Your Identity

- Reflect on the identity you wrote down in Chapter 2. How has it evolved since then?

___

- Think about how the habits you've built have contributed to this identity.

___

- Write down your plan for continuing to build habits that align with your desired identity and make them a core part of who you are.

Chapter 14:
The Habits of High Performers

- Research and identify the habits of high performers in your field or industry.

_____
_____
_____
_____
_____
_____
_____
_____
_____
_____
_____
_____
_____
_____
_____
_____
_____

- Choose one or two of these habits to incorporate into your own routine.

_____
_____
_____
_____
_____
_____
_____
_____
_____

- Write down your plan for integrating these habits into your daily life and tracking your progress.

Chapter 15:
How to Build Habits That Last Forever

- Think about one habit you want to build that you want to last forever.

_____
_____
_____
_____
_____
_____
_____
_____
_____
_____
_____
_____
_____
_____
_____
_____
_____
_____
_____

- Write down your plan for continuing to practice this habit for the long term, including strategies for staying motivated and adapting to changing circumstances.

_____
_____
_____
_____
_____
_____
_____

MAKE A HABIT SCORESHEET

Who determines what is a habit?

Over time, we have developed habits out of our instinctive activities. Repeatedly carrying out a task makes it automatic and imprinted in our brains.
James Clear defines a habit as an action that is repeated often enough to become automatic.

1 make a list of your daily activities.

Make a list of all the routine activities you perform without giving them a second thought, such as getting out of bed, brushing your teeth, checking your phone, taking a shower, drinking coffee, etc.

_____
_____
_____
_____
_____
_____
_____
_____
_____
_____
_____
_____
_____
_____
_____
_____
_____

2 On the next page Determine if each action is a positive, detrimental, or neutral habit.

Put a plus sign (+) next to a habit if you think it's helpful and will be helpful to you in the long run.

Put a "-" next to anything that is a bad habit or will have long-term negative effects.
The behavior should have a "=" next to it if it is neutral.

3 Be conscious of your habits.

Nothing needs to be changed at first. Simply observing what is truly happening is the aim. Without judging or criticizing yourself, pay attention to your thoughts and behaviors.

The key goal is for you to become aware of your habits and the circumstances that cause them. As a consequence, it will be simpler for you to identify the behaviors that need to be altered and to react in a way that is in your best interests.

HABITS SCORESHEET

Habits	Good habit	Bad habit	Neutral habits

WHO YOU ARE

Your habits shape who you are, and vice versa.

The following are the three phases of behavior change:

- a change in your outcomes (what you acquire or accomplish)
- a change in your behavior (what you do)
- or identity (what you believe)

Simply said, your present behaviors mirror who you are right now. Your behavior reveals the type of person you believe yourself to be, whether consciously or unconsciously. If you want to alter your behavior (i.e., the things you think about yourself), you must first change who you are.

The best way to change your habits is to concentrate on whom you want to become rather than what you want to achieve. Add the behavior to your revised self-perception.

It merely requires two simple steps: selecting the identity you wish to assume. You may prove yourself by securing little triumphs.

What sort of individual could be able to assist you in achieving your objectives? So, be that person.

Although they can, habits are significant because they can change how you view yourself, not because they can make you more successful.

Write a brief description of who you are at this moment in the first column of the table below. Sort the ideas you've described into positive and negative groups

POSITIVE BELIEFS

s/n	Who am I today	Who do I want to be?

NEGATIVE BELIEFS

s/n	Who am I today	Who do I want to be?

Imagine yourself in a serene setting, becoming the person you want to be. Please describe this individual in the second column above.

Analyze the myths given above. Enter up to three negative opinions about yourself in the table below. For example, I lack the willpower to change my eating habits. Make note of any misconceptions about who you are that are based on how others see you.

Describe how you want to change each belief

Negative Beliefs

Identify three negative assumptions you have about yourself.	How are you going to alter each belief?	Is this opinion formed based on the way people see you? Is it real?

List the habits you need to develop or give up in order to transform into the person you desire for yourself.

Prioritize developing these habits.

Choose the habit you want to work on first. The perfect habit is one that doesn't take much work at first but has a big impact over time.

The habits I must develop in order to be the kind of person I want to be	Order of Priority

The behavior you intend to adopt

Take into account a new habit that will change your life but is difficult for you to adopt or an old habit that you can't manage to kick. Ideally, this should be the action you prioritized on the previous page.

This workbook will help you develop or break that negative habit.

Name the modification you want.

_____
_____
_____
_____
_____
_____
_____
_____
_____
_____
_____
_____
_____
_____

How would your life change if you are successful?

_____
_____
_____
_____
_____
_____

Identify the challenges you've faced while attempting to develop this habit in the past.

Why will things be different this time? How can you overcome difficulties you've already encountered?

Break THE HABIT INTO SMALL BITES.

Break the habit into small chunks.

For instance, you may decide what, how often, and when to eat, how to cook your meals, and what items to keep on hand if you want to develop good eating habits.

Determine the little modifications that each component needs in order to succeed.

Habits:	COMPONENTS	CHANGES YOU NEED TO MAKE

How Do Habits Develop?

Habit:			
Trigger	Craving	Response	Reward

Every habit follows a similar process even while not all habits benefit our health, the process is the same for both habits.

Using the table above, describe the cue, trigger, reaction, and reward for the habit you have chosen to focus on.

Trigger

Habits begin with a signal or a stimulus to act. For instance, entering a dark space drives you to move in a way that will improve your vision.

Craving

Then comes the need for a state transition. in our case, to be able to view.

Response

Our response or action comes next. Switching on the light in our case.

Reward

The goal of every habit is the reward, which comes at the end of the process. Having the ability to observe your environment in this situation. A positive feedback loop was established if receiving the prize made you feel content. That indicates

Follow your brain's guidance the next time this signal arises to get the same result. You start doing this routine automatically after you repeat it frequently enough. Habits are established in this manner.

Have you ever had coffee in the morning consistently? When you initially wake up, that is your cue to feel aware. In reaction, you choose to get out of bed and prepare a cup of coffee. Your reward is that you're awake.

Using the table from the previous page, list the cue, trigger, reaction, and reward related to the habit you have decided to focus on.

_____
_____
_____
_____
_____
_____
_____
_____
_____
_____
_____
_____
_____
_____

FORMING NEW HABITS: A GUIDE

There are four rules for altering behavior:

1. The First Law of Obviousness

Making indications as explicit as you can increases your likelihood of acting upon them.

Everybody has specific actions that they are triggered to engage in. Because some triggers can lead to habitual behavior, you can use this to change your habits. You may, for instance, change your environment to encourage better practices. If you want to exercise more regularly, keep your gym clothes and running shoes in a place you won't forget.

If you want to consume healthier food, place your chopped vegetables on the visible shelf when you open your refrigerator rather than hiding them in the vegetable drawer.

Don't linger in seductive situations. It is easier to resist temptation than to avoid it.

What might you do to make it crystal clear:

_____
_____
_____
_____
_____
_____
_____

STACK YOUR ACTIONS

Choose an existing daily habit and layer your fresh habit on top of it. This is known as habit stacking. For example, every morning after cleaning my teeth, I perform yoga.

How can you use habit stacking to integrate a new habit with an old one?
I'll follow [existing habit] with [new habit].

Use implementation intentions (a detailed plan of action indicating when and where you'll practice the habit you wish to develop).

If you want to form new habits, you must have a well-defined plan of action. You can't just say, "I'm going to start working out," and expect it to happen.

Follow through. Instead, say, "I'll exercise for 20 minutes at 7 a.m. on Sunday, Tuesday, and Thursday."

An implementation intention specifies a particular action plan, including where and when you want to practice the habit. According to studies, doing so is the most effective approach to form a new habit.

Action plan

WHEN	
WHERE	
WHAT	

2. Make it Attractive, 2nd Law

Since individuals are driven by the prospect of earning a reward, making habits appealing will help you maintain them.

Our brain releases dopamine, a hormone that makes us feel good, when we take part in rewarding activities. However, dopamine is also released when we plan to perform these behaviors, in addition to when we actually perform them. As a result, planning a trip is enjoyable and engaging in and of itself.

We may take advantage of this while attempting to form new behaviors. If we can turn a habit into something enjoyable, we will be far more likely to stick with it and complete our goals. James Clear suggests "temptation bundling" to do this. The process of temptation bundling, which will make your brain produce dopamine, occurs when you link a negative activity you wish to engage in with a positive one. Make a decision, for example, to only watch TV when working out on the treadmill—either in general or a favorite show.

How can you make your habit more desirable?

_____
_____
_____
_____
_____
_____
_____
_____
_____
_____
_____
_____
_____

How may temptation bundling be used to your advantage?

3. Third Law: Make it Simple

If you want to build a new habit, try to make it as easy as possible to pick up.

Of course, we'll prefer the one that requires the least amount of work. Making acts as easy as feasible is therefore essential if you want them to stick as habits. Create an environment that will encourage doing the right thing as much as you can. James Clear gives some guidance on how to gradually simplify behaviors.

DESIRE TO MINIMIZE FRACTION

If you want to do anything, make sure the tools are available so there is no friction. If you want to go for a run, for example, keep your running clothes out. If you don't want to waste time on your phone, turn it off or avoid having it nearby while you are working. You'll build up enough resilience this way that you'll only use it when absolutely necessary.

THE TWO-MINUTE RULE

According to the "Two-Minute Rule," it shouldn't take more than two minutes to form a new habit.

This is another way to make any new undertaking appear doable. The guideline recognizes that beginning something is always the first and most important step. If you want to run, limit your time to two minutes at a time. Once you start running, you'll probably keep going.

Make your habits rewarding as soon as possible to help you alter your behavior.

Making new habits delightful is the key to modifying behavior. This can be difficult because our routines are typically beneficial in the long term even though we don't feel fulfilled right away. For instance, exercising consistently over time will result in improved fitness, albeit we won't notice the improvement immediately away. On the other hand, unhealthy behaviors usually do offer an immediate reward, such as the enjoyment of eating chocolate.

Try to link your new behaviors to some sort of immediate enjoyment in order to develop good long-term habits. For instance, if you want to start losing weight, start saving for a purchase you truly want to make. To save money for something you truly want, put a dollar (or whichever much you decide) into the savings account each day that you work out and/or eat properly. You will now experience a momentary delight whenever you deposit money into your account. This will support your continued progress as you work toward achieving your long-term goals.

The laws previously discussed dealt with forming new habits. The following are tips for quitting harmful habits.

1: Make your hints difficult to notice.

Everybody has specific actions that they are triggered to engage in. The buzz of your phone, for instance, serves as a reminder to check your messages. If you find yourself spending a lot of time on social media or on your phone while working, move it away from you or put it on silent.

The best strategy for beating temptation is to avoid it. How do the reasons behind your harmful behaviors get hidden? If you want to change your eating habits, don't keep junk food at your home or at work, for example.

2 render undesirable harmful behaviors

Focus on the benefits of stopping your unhealthy behaviors to make them appear unwanted.

When we associate habits with positive feelings, they are desirable; when we associate them with unpleasant emotions, they are repulsive.
You may develop a motivating ritual by doing something delightful just before a difficult habit.

3. Make the bad behavior as difficult as you can.

INTENT TO AMEND FRACTION

For instance, switch off your phone or avoid having it nearby when you are working if you don't want to waste time on it. You'll build up enough resilience this way that you'll only use it when absolutely necessary.

APPLY THE "TWO-MINUTE RULE"

The two-minute rule can be employed to make it seem possible to refrain from doing something. For instance, if you're on a diet and you're desiring chocolate, indulge for two minutes in your favorite pastime. If you don't immediately sate your hunger, it won't last more than two minutes.

I will:

_____
_____
_____

_____
_____
_____
_____
_____
_____
_____
_____
_____
_____
_____
_____
_____

USE A TOOL TO COMMIT TO SOMETHING

You are making a choice right now that will ensure better behavior down the road. For instance, if you want to save money, you may enroll in an automatic savings plan.

"Using technology to automate your behaviors is the most reliable and effective strategy to ensure the appropriate behavior."

I will:
_____
_____
_____
_____
_____
_____
_____
_____
_____

_____
_____
_____
_____

4 Make your daily activities uncomfortable.

The main rule for behavior modification is to make unwanted actions uncomfortable. This can be difficult since unhealthy behaviors, like the pleasure of eating chocolate, can give an immediate high while eventually being unsatisfactory.

Attach a small amount of immediate satisfaction to quitting a harmful habit.

Consider making a $1 (or other amounts you choose) deposit into a savings account for every day you refrain from a bad habit. You will now experience a momentary delight whenever you deposit money into your account. This will support your continued progress as you work toward achieving your long-term goals.

The Four Laws of Habits Change

To Form a Good Habit	To Break a Bad Habit	How can you do this?
Make it obvious	Make it invisible	
Make it attractive	Make it unattractive	
Make it easy	Make it difficult	
Make it satisfying	Make it unsatisfying	

MINDFULNESS

Autopilot

We may react to some circumstances impulsively without really thinking about them. For instance, you can mindlessly consume junk food when attempting to develop good eating habits.
Practicing mindfulness is one way to stop this. When you would normally be on autopilot, try to be present.
Describe a bad habit you have that you engage in automatically or unconsciously as a result of it has embedded itself in your being.

What emotions does this evoke in you?

_____
_____
_____
_____
_____
_____
_____
_____
_____
_____
_____
_____
_____
_____
_____

How do you avoid acting automatically? I will:

_____
_____
_____
_____
_____
_____
_____
_____
_____
_____
_____
_____

Make a list of methods for sustaining mindfulness and awareness of your actions.

_____
_____
_____
_____
_____
_____
_____
_____
_____
_____
_____
_____

PERSONAL SETTINGS

One of the factors that influence our habits and behavior is our surroundings. Retailers display items they want us to buy at eye level because visual signals have a big influence on our behavior. The formation of habits might begin with a signal. We should thus arrange our surroundings such that we can notice the items that are related to those actions if we wish to improve our behavior and habits. If you want to exercise more, for instance, put your workout gear wherever you will see it. If you want to eat more veggies, place them in the refrigerator at eye level.

How can you make your environment conducive to the development of a habit?

I will:

_____
_____
_____
_____
_____
_____
_____
_____
_____
_____
_____
_____
_____
_____

How could you make your cues clearer? I will:

_____
_____
_____

Set up your surroundings right away. Describe the changes you made.

FRIENDS AND FAMILY

The Impact of Your Family and Friends on Your Habits
We typically adopt the traditions of three different social groups: the close-knit (family and friends), the large (tribe), and the influential (those with status and prestige).

One of the best methods to form healthy habits is to integrate into a society where your desired behavior is the norm and you already have something in common with the group.
If a behavior can get us respect, acceptance, and praise, we find it attractive. Look for others who have been successful in creating the same habit, and pay attention to their suggestions.

Make a list of what you can change or achieve. For each item on your list, indicate what you think is manageable and what will make it work. If you need a list of activities, for instance, add a list of simple exercises you love doing. You can provide a YouTube video link for each workout.

I will:

_____
_____
_____
_____
_____
_____
_____
_____
_____
_____
_____
_____

What emotions does this evoke in you?

_____
_____
_____
_____
_____
_____

How do you avoid acting automatically? I will:

_____
_____
_____
_____
_____
_____
_____
_____
_____
_____
_____

Make a list of methods for sustaining mindfulness and awareness of your actions.

_____
_____
_____
_____
_____
_____
_____
_____
_____

Conclusion

- Reflect on your overall experience with the workbook journal and the Atomic Habits book.

_____
_____
_____
_____
_____
_____
_____
_____
_____
_____
_____
_____
_____
_____
_____
_____
_____

- Write down your biggest takeaways and any new habits you've built or old habits you've broken as a result of the exercises in this journal.

_____
_____
_____
_____
_____
_____
_____
_____
_____
_____
_____

- Commit to continuing to prioritize small habits and incremental progress in your personal and professional life.

Made in the USA
Las Vegas, NV
03 June 2024